YOUR KNOWLEDGE HAS VALUE

AF148958

Bibliographic information published by the German National Library:

The German National Library lists this publication in the National Bibliography; detailed bibliographic data are available on the Internet at http://dnb.dnb.de .

Imprint:

Copyright © 2010 GRIN Verlag
Print and binding: Books on Demand GmbH, Norderstedt Germany
ISBN: 9783640805730

This book at GRIN:

https://www.grin.com/document/165075

Felix Jeschonnek

Detective Mystery in the School Story - The Example of Harry Potter and the Chamber of Secrets

GRIN Verlag

GRIN - Your knowledge has value

Since its foundation in 1998, GRIN has specialized in publishing academic texts by students, college teachers and other academics as e-book and printed book. The website www.grin.com is an ideal platform for presenting term papers, final papers, scientific essays, dissertations and specialist books.

Visit us on the internet:

http://www.grin.com/

http://www.facebook.com/grincom

http://www.twitter.com/grin_com

Detective Mystery in the School Story

The Example of Joanne K. Rowling's Harry Potter and the Chamber of Secrets

Felix Jeschonnek

KGS Hemmingen

Seminarfach sf11

Schuljahr 2009/2010

2.Halbjahr (Q2)

Facharbeit

Vorgelegt am 5. März 2010

Content

Detective Mystery in the School Story
The Example of *Harry Potter and the Chamber of Secrets*

1. Introduction
1.1. Assumption

J. K. Rowling's famous Harry Potter series which started with *Harry Potter and the Philosopher's Stone* in 1997 is commonly known as a fantasy story. This is due to the fact that its most striking aspect is magic which is a typical sign for an ordinary fantasy novel. Accordingly, there has to be something more important than magic in the story in order to make it as popular, interesting and fascinating as it is. Of course magic is highly important for Harry Potter's popularity and to make a difference between the series and any other school story. Without magic the series would probably have been less popular than it is now, since it would not have been something special.

The story is neither only a fantasy story nor is it only a school story. It is something less striking that is -at least- as important as magic for the series. In the following Detective Mystery will be explained and revealed as one of the most important elements of *Harry Potter and the Chamber of Secrets*. Moreover this paper seeks to prove that magic is not even necessary for the story itself.

Magic is a minor aspect of *Harry Potter and the Chamber of Secrets* and even unimportant compared to Detective Mystery.

1.2. Genre

The Harry Potter series unites many genres. The world in which the action takes place is presented as our world from Harry's point of view who gets to know the world of magic by learning that he is a wizard and has to go to the Hogwarts School of Witchcraft and Wizardry. This is the point where the story becomes fantastic.

Due to the fact that Harry spends most of his time in school, the story could be classified as a School Story, as well. Moreover, Hogwarts is not only a school for him. It is the place where he belongs, the place he wants himself to be. (comp. Rowling 1998:22)

Those two are the most obvious genres the Harry Potter series is part of but indeed not the most important ones. The story of the series is build upon fantasy, magic and of course it mostly takes place in a school but the whole story grounds on a murder which is a presupposition and thus a typical sign for a detective novel. (comp. Van Dine pseud. for Willard Huntington Wright 1928:rule 7) It is the murder on Harry's parents and the attempted murder on Harry by Lord Voldemort that triggered the following events. That is to say that the story would not be possible without this crime.

2. Detective Mystery

2.1. Definition and Derivation

Detective Mystery is basically a synonym for Detective Fiction which includes essential elements of the literally Mystery. The literally Mystery is based on solving a riddle of some kind. It is to say that something is characterised as a mystery when there is something that is hidden, unknown or only not normal.

The focus in Mystery Fiction lays on the act of finding the hidden part and the missing information, "it highlights two forms of enigma, Who and How, with especial emphasis on the former" (Malmgren 2001:20) this is the striking aspect of this kind of literature. Moreover, it is the occasion for the term "whodunit" which is a common substitute for the classification Mystery Fiction. So Detective Mystery connects the pure riddle to the person who tries to solve it. The detective himself is one essential part of the story and the riddle he has to deal with is the other one. By emphasising his personal feelings and thoughts the story can become more touching. This helps to make the story attractive to a bigger audience due to the fact that in a traditional Mystery Novel "the emphasis was on investigation and only incidental concerned with characterization and human emotion" (Schwartz 1989:3) Subsequently, the character of the protagonist can be developed even better by using devices of Detective Fiction.

One criteria for a Mystery Fiction novel is a "centred world [...] a world which has a centre, an anchor, a ground" so that "effects can be connected to causes, where external signs can be connected to internal conditions." (Malmgren 2001:13)

That implies that the main part of the story, in other words the investigation process, usually takes place in a limited and manageable area, e.g. a summer residence which is, at least in Mystery Fiction, always far from any semblance of civilisation as, for example, in *At the Villa Rose* by A. E. W. Mason.

This centred world is also necessary to make it easier for the reader to follow or to investigate on his own. Both, Mystery Fiction and Detective Fiction, are predestined to create a kind of interaction with the reader. Crime Fiction in general allows the reader to make up his own theories, to investigate on his own or -literally- to become the detective. Thus, protagonists in Crime Fiction are supposed to be special, either physical or mental, in order to make it easier for the reader to identify.

2.2. The Protagonist in a Detective Story

As it has already been mentioned that the Detective has to be special in a certain way but being special does not necessarily mean being more powerful. Indeed the protagonists have to be able to acquit "themselves well in one-on-one competitions, such as shooting, fist fighting [...] and the verbal joust" (Marling 2009:*The Hero/Heroine*) but usually protagonists were both, able to defend themselves against everyone or everything and invested with special features.

The reader experiences the story from the detective's point of view. That is why the hero can gain emotional meaning. The detective becomes a part of the reader because he is his only connection to the story. One sees trough his eyes, one hears with his ears so he is (literally) used to let the reader become part of the story. Thus, the reader feels bound with him and shares his feelings, fears and hopes concerning anything that could possibly happen to the hero. This connection is growing stronger as the main character learns more about the crime e.g. about the suspected, the perpetrators, the motivations or what has actually happened. The reader is completely involved in the investigation process. So while the detective gains information and learns more about the crime, the reader gets to know the protagonist and learns more about his feelings.

> Treating victim and criminal without much emotional interest or complexity places the detective story's primary emphasis on those characters who are investigating the crime, the most important of which is the detective. (Malmgren 2001:36)

2.3. Assistants, Enemies and False Suspects

Indeed the story basically grounds on the detective himself and the investigation process which presupposes murderer and victim. There are already three categories of characters; detectives, murderers and victims but there is still a fourth one. (comp. Cawelti 1977:96)

This consists of those characters who are involved with the crime but need the detective's aid to solve it. It includes three main types: [...],the friends or assistants of the detective who frequently chronicle his exploits;[...] [and] the collection of false suspects [...] (Cawelti 1977:96)

Those two categories are different in attitude towards the detective, importance for crime/story and, of course, constancy. Constancy, in this case, means weather they are part of every crime or investigating process or if they appear just once. It is common for two kinds of characters to be part of every or at least more than only one story; the detective's friends/assistants and an archenemy.

The friend or assistant can be seen as a part of the protagonist himself, due to the fact that the detective usually talks to him in in order to detect the missing information. Hence, the friend/assistant is a handy device to show the detection of the crime. The author can change the detective's interior monologue, which is necessary to let the reader know what is going on in the protagonist whilst thinking, to a dialogue which makes it not only easier to follow, it can also be more entertaining because of the second personality which comes into play. However, the friend's/assistant's main idea or task is to make clear what goes on in the detective's mind.

A special status is taken by the archenemy or antagonist who is easy to characterise as the evil side of the protagonist, literally, his opposite. He does not have to appear in every novel (if there is a series about one detective), but he is a weighty ankle of the whole situation the protagonist has to deal with. He is the one who is equipollent to the protagonist thus he is always able to do harm to him or to give him a hard time. He is the one the hero has in mind, always. That is why he does not have to be part of every single story. Just the possibility that he might be involved in the mystery, is enough to make him a permanent side of the detective and the series.

The false suspects, as well as the real suspects, held up the interaction in the novel and the reader's emotional interest in it. The interaction is hold up because these people build up the story which forms the framework. Without them, there would be no use for a detective, thus no novel. Suspects and false suspects are used to cause pity, anger, sadness or anything else the reader could possibly feel. People from this category can appear, disappear, be killed and rescued without significant meaning for the rest of the series. For example; killing the protagonist just in order to cause pity would make it impossible to go on with the story. Whereas there would not be a problem if the author would let a congenial man or woman die who could have also been according to evidences or false ones, even if unlikely, the murderer, but an emotion would have also been triggered and the reader would feel part of the story, by sharing some character's feelings.

3. The Example of *Harry Potter and the Chamber of Secrets*

3.1. The Murder

Harry's world is build up on magic, but that does not necessarily mean that the story would not work out well without it. It is the most obvious ankle of the series that Harry is a sorcerer's apprentice who is thrown right into a new world, full of magic, fascinating gadgets and further fantastic items. However, everything is new to him in the beginning but gets somewhat boring, soon. He simply gets used to it by reason that he is surrounded by magic all day. Being a wizard is hardly anything special, if everyone else is, too. There is just one thing that makes a striking difference between Harry and the other pupils at Hogwarts. It is a scar on his forehead that makes Harry "so particularly unusual, even for a wizard." It is "the only hint of Harry's mysterious past" or, to be more specific, the only -obvious- reminder that Harry had [...] survived a curse from the greatest dark sorcerer of all time, Lord Voldemort. Since the day he survived the attack, he is famous without knowing about it, due to the fact that he did not know anything about the wizarding world until his eleventh birthday.

So even if the whole world in the Harry Potter series grounds on magic the story and the following events are a result from his parent's violent death and his survival. Except from how Lord Voldemort killed Harry's parents it had nothing to do with magic. Voldemort committed the crime with the aid of supernatural powers but his motivation was to stay alive and to remain the only one in power. Accordingly, the murder could rather be seen as a political crime, as a method to stabilise someone's leading position. By coincidence, Voldemort figured out that Harry would be the only one to kill him. So he tried to protect himself from what was going to happen if Harry stayed alive. Voldemort fails to killing Harry and, in the beginning, nobody knew why that is why it is at least under special circumstances just a mysterious crime, which is the presupposition for a Detective Mystery story.

As soon as Harry has become a part of the magic society he starts collecting information. He tries to find out as much as possible about his family and his parent's death because of his small knowledge about his parents. The wizarding world is also interesting to Harry, but it is mainly a connection to his parents. He gets to know people who were his parent's friends or even confidants. After that, he starts to think about the information on his own and reveals his parents situation. Harry tries to understand why his parents had to die and what Voldemort tried to achieve by killing them. This personal concern in the crime triggers Harry's development into a detective and this is where the series becomes a detective story. After all that is clear the reader can focus on the detection.

3.2. The Mystery

It is not only the whole series, even the single books ground on several mysteries. There is always the superordinate concern which is basically a question (Why did Voldemort do it?), but there are also the smaller ones which are connected to the main question. These smaller riddles are a part of the great mystery and the solutions can help to understand, but in the beginning of every book there is no obvious connection to what has happened once.

> "'If Harry Potter goes back to Hogwarts, he will be in mortal danger.' [...] 'There is a plot, Harry Potter. A plot to make most terrible things happen at Hogwarts School of Witchcraft and Wizardry this year,' [...]." (Rowling 1998:22)

This warning, given by Dobby, is the first riddle Harry has to deal with in *Harry Potter and the Chamber of Secrets*. This warning brings up two questions; "What terrible things?" and "Who's plotting them?" (Rowling 1998: 22/23) These are the questions Harry gets to answer in the second part of the book, but also the slightly changed standard questions of Detective Mystery. The second riddle he has to think about is, why he and Ron could not get through the barrier between platform nine and ten, even though Ron's family got through, the minute before. (comp. Rowling 1998: 77) As Harry and Ron will find out later, it was Dobby who closed the barrier in order to prevent Harry from going back to Hogwarts. So, even the small riddles are connected to other small ones and, thus, the whole mystery could be compared to a puzzle. It needs the small pieces to fall in place to clarify the whole image.

Another mystery which is also an important trigger for the investigation is the opening of the Chamber of Secrets. Again, it arises two questions; Who opened it and why? This is the first mystery which is directly related to Harry's archenemy Voldemort. Harry and his friends try to find out who the heir is and what it means, that the Chamber of Secrets is open. (comp. Rowling 1998:151)

Although, Harry is drawing conclusions to the great mystery later in the novel, the story starts with small noticeable problems which mostly happen to be right before school or soon after school has started. Sometimes, there are several events which seem to be disjointed at first sight.

3.3. The Investigation

This is the "real source of mystery at the centre of the Harry Potter novels [....]. Harry and his friends [...] solve mysteries of mistaken identity and uncover the perpetrators of evil deeds." (Routledge 2001:3) Investigation as the main part of Detective Mystery is the core of the whole novel whereas magic is not superfluous but still not necessary for the plot.

As already mentioned, the Mysteries have a connection to Harry's antagonist, Lord Voldemort, who is his arch-enemy, but not the only one. Harry has another enemy among the pupils. This school-enemy is Draco Malfoy. Harry blames him to be the heir, thus he holds him responsible for the attacks which happen after the Chamber has been opened. They, Harry, Ron and Hermione, try "to get a confession out of Malfoy" as soon as possible, by use of the Polyjuice Potion. (Rowling 1998:200) Malfoy's character cannot easily be classified as suspect, because of his relation to Harry, as an enemy. They try to play a trick on him, to prove his fault, but they will find out that it is not him who seeks to kill Muggle-born witches and wizards, even if he appreciates it. Therefor, it is necessary to think about other possible delinquents. This should be a reachable aim due to three points.

The first point is, that there are the 'typical suspects' in every Harry Potter novel. Even if the typical ones are almost always the false ones, they do not change. Malfoy, for example, is one of Harry's 'favourite' suspects, because of his behaviour towards him and his friends. He simply dislikes him and no matter what he does, it could be seen as the preparation of a crime, from Harry's point of view. Malfoy is connected to the crimes somehow, but not as much as Harry usually expects him to be. In *The Chamber of Secrets* it was his father who slipped Ginny Weasley Voldemort's diary secretly. (comp. Rowling 1998:161)

The second point is, that Hogwarts represents exactly the centred world a Mystery Fiction novel needs. The people are limited concerning flexibility, in other words, where to go and what to do, especially the pupils. Hogwarts is totally isolated from the rest of the wizarding world. It is easier to detect mysteries in the school this way even if the inspectors themselves are limited in agitation. All that "limit[s] the suspects to a number that can be dealt with efficiently." (Velardi 2009:2) Thus, focusing on suspects from one certain group -Slytherin- is a common technique to ease the investigation in Crime Fiction.

The third one is the fact that there are hints in the whole novel, which are in almost every Detective Mystery Story only to allow the reader to find the solution without reading the final chapter. In *The Chamber of Secrets* the first hint, for example, is given by Dobby. When Dobby visits Harry at home to warn him, Harry asks him, if Voldemort has something to do with the plot. Dobby answers that it has nothing to do with "He-Who-Must-Not-Be-Named".(Rowling 1998:23) He did not say, that it has nothing to do with Voldemort. His "eyes where wide and he seemed to be trying to give Harry a hint." (Rowling 1998:23) He tries to make Harry think about the meaning of the term by widening his eyes, due to the fact that he is not allowed to 'say' who is involved.

The investigation in *The Chamber of Secrets* works exactly like the investigation usually works in any other Detective Story.

3.4. The Detective

Harry is one of the "most common detective['s], a gentleman amateur, [who] is the central character in mystery fiction" (Velardi 2009:2), but his assistants are not less essential. Due to the fact that there are two of them, it is easier to collect information and to form theories which can be proved or disproved, later. The hero in the novel shows every attribute of a detective in a Detective Mystery. He is special even for the special ones (the magicians), he is usually calm, but can be really upset and active. Moreover, he is polite and frugal. In the beginning he is the inexperienced nice-guy who develops a character and sees life.

All in all, it is to say, that Harry is a detective with supernatural powers in a world where being supernatural is normal. His sense of justice and his personal interest make him such a good detective. The mysteries he has to deal with are sometimes cruel, strange, hard to retrace, creative and so are the crimes in *Harry Potter and the Chamber of Secrets*. Harry is not only a wizard but even more important -by reason that nearly anybody is a magician- also a successful and flexible junior detective.

4. Conclusion

Harry Potter and the Chamber of Secrets definitely bears striking elements of Detective Mystery it is even certain that the whole series could easily be classified as "Detective Mystery" or "Crime Fiction" because of the fact that it meets the criteria. Indeed, this genres would be in line with the plot but there is more about the classification than just the literary techniques and forms. The combination of magic and a public school makes the series as popular and interesting as it is. That is to say that even if the assumption is right, the classification as "Crime Fiction/Detective Mystery" would be hard to understand for the reader. So, it is just practical to make the book a fantasy novel.

As already alluded to, the assumption is partly right. The series grounds on Detective Mystery and it is the most important element of the plot. It would be possible, of course with some slight changes, to keep the plot if magic was not be part of the story even if it would have bad consequences for its popularity. It is the main aspect, but the Harry Potter series is a combination of many genres and this combination is more important than any of the single elements.

Bibliography:

Cavelti, J. G. - *Adventure, Mystery and Romance*. Chicago: University of Chicago Press, 1977

Malmgren, C. D. - *Anatomy of Murder: Mystery, Detective and Crime Fiction*. Bowling Green: Bowling Green State University Popular Press, 2001

Marling, W. - *Dashiell Hammett* (detnovel.com, (20.02.2010) web), 2009 (http://www.detnovel.com/Hero-Heroine.html)

Mason, A.E.W. - *At the Villa Rose*, 1910

Rowling, J. K. - *Harry Potter and the Chamber of Secrets*. London: Bloomsbury Publishing, 1998

Routledge, C. – *Harry Potter and the Mystery of Ordinary Life*. In Gavin, Adrienne and Christopher Routledge (eds.) *Mystery in Chlidren's Literature:From the Rational to the Supernatural*. Basingstoke: Palgrave, 2001 pp. 202-209.

Schwartz, R. – *Mystery and Detective Fiction: Comparison and Contrast*. Yale -New Haven University 1989

(http://www.yale.edu/ynhti/curriculum/units/1989/4/89.04.08.x.html)

Van Dine, S. S. (pseud. For Wright, Willard Huntington) - *Twenty Rules for writing Detective Stories*. New York: American Magazine, 1928

Velardi, P. A. - *Plot, Character and Settings: A Study of Mystery and Detective Fiction*. Yale-New Haven University, 2010

(http://www.yale.edu/ynhti/curriculum/units/1989/4/89.04.09.x.html)

YOUR KNOWLEDGE HAS VALUE